ROBINSON CRUSOE

NOTES

including
- *Life of the Author*
- *General Plot Summary*
- *Summaries and Commentaries*
- *Questions for Review*

by
Cynthia McGowan, M.A.
University of Nebraska

INCORPORATED

LINCOLN, NEBRASKA 68501

Editor

Gary Carey, M.A.
University of Colorado

Consulting Editor

James L. Roberts, Ph.D.
Department of English
University of Nebraska

Cliffs Notes, Inc.   Lincoln, Nebraska

CONTENTS

Robinson Crusoe Notes

LIFE OF THE AUTHOR

Defoe's early life was not easy. He was born about 1660 in London to a poor, but hard-working butcher who was, in addition, a Dissenter from the Church of England. Because his father was a Dissenter, Daniel was unable to attend such traditional and prestigious schools as Oxford and Cambridge; instead, he had to attend a Dissenting academy, where he studied science and the humanities, preparing to become a Presbyterian minister. It was not long, however, before he decided against the ministry. Living for the rest of his life in the strict confines of a parish seemed stifling. Daniel recognized his independent, ambitious nature and wanted to be a part of the rapidly growing business world of London. So, after a short apprenticeship, he decided to set up his own haberdashery shop in a fashionable section of London.

Not only did Defoe prove that he had a flair for business, but he also tried his talents in yet another field: politics. England, in 1685, was ruled by James Stuart, a Catholic, who was strongly anti-Protestant. Defoe was a staunch believer in religious freedom and, during the next three years, he published several pamphlets protesting against the king's policies. This in itself was risky, but Defoe was never a man to be stopped when he felt strongly about an issue. Shortly thereafter, James Stuart was deposed, and Defoe held several part-time advisory positions under the new king.

In 1962, the economic boom that had created many rich men and increased employment suddenly collapsed. Foreign trade came to a sudden halt when war was declared with France. Among the many men whose fortunes disappeared was Daniel Defoe. Then, after several years of trying to pay off his debts, Defoe suffered another setback: King William died, and Defoe, still a fierce Dissenter, found himself persecuted once again. And, after he published a particularly sharp political satire, he found himself quartered in Newgate Prison for three months. He was finally released, but he had yet another ordeal to endure; he was fastened in a public pillory for three days.

When Defoe returned home, he found a failing business and a family wracked by poverty. His money gone, his family destitute, and his own health deteriorated, it is little wonder that Defoe compromised his principles and pledged to support his foremost adversary, Queen Anne.

Newly sworn to the Tory party, Defoe was soon writing again. Ironically, he began publishing a newspaper that was used for propaganda purposes by one of Queen Anne's chief politicians, a man who had been instrumental in Defoe's imprisonment. But Defoe could not silence his true political feelings and, several years later, he published several pamphlets and spent several more months in Newgate Prison. A year later, Defoe was arrested because of another political writing, but this time he avoided Newgate.

Defoe then tried a new tactic: he began secretly writing for his own party's journal, while publishing essays for the Tory journal.

In 1719, Defoe finished and published *Robinson Crusoe,* a long, imaginative literary masterpiece. It was popular with the public and has never lost its appeal to adventure and romance. Other novels soon followed, in addition to his multitude of articles and essays. But debts still plagued Defoe, and he died at 70, hiding in a boarding house, trying to evade a bill collector.

GENERAL PLOT SUMMARY

Robinson Crusoe, as a young and impulsive wanderer, defied his parents and went to sea. He was involved in a series of violent storms at sea and was warned by the captain that he should not be a seafaring man. Ashamed to go home, Crusoe boarded another ship and returned from a successful trip to Africa. Taking off again, Crusoe met with bad luck and was taken prisoner in Sallee. His captors sent Crusoe out to fish, and he used this to his advantage and escaped, along with a slave.

He was rescued by a Portuguese ship and started a new adventure. He landed in Brazil, and, after some time, he became the owner of a sugar plantation. Hoping to increase his wealth by buying slaves, he aligned himself with other planters and undertook a trip to Africa in order to bring back a shipload of slaves. After surviving a storm, Crusoe and the others were shipwrecked. He was thrown upon shore only to discover that he was the sole survivor of the wreck.

Crusoe made immediate plans for food, and then shelter, to protect himself from wild animals. He brought as many things as possible from the wrecked ship, things that would be useful later to him. In addition, he began to develop talents that he had never used in order to provide himself with necessities. Cut off from the company of men, he began to communicate with God, thus beginning the first part of his religious conversion. To keep his sanity and to entertain himself, he began a journal. In the journal, he recorded every task that he performed each day since he had been marooned.

As time passed, Crusoe became a skilled craftsman, able to construct many useful things, and thus furnished himself with diverse comforts. He also learned about farming, as a result of some seeds which he brought with him. An illness prompted some prophetic dreams, and Crusoe began to reappraise his duty to God. Crusoe explored his island and discovered another part of the island much richer and more fertile, and he built a summer home there.

One of the first tasks he undertook was to build himself a canoe in case an escape became possible, but the canoe was too heavy to get to the water. He then constructed a small boat and journeyed around the island. Crusoe reflected on his earlier, wicked life, disobeying his parents, and wondered if it might be related to his isolation on this island.

After spending about fifteen years on the island, Crusoe found a man's naked footprint, and he was sorely beset by apprehensions, which kept him awake many nights. He considered many possibilities to account for the footprint and he began to take extra precautions against a possible intruder. Sometime later, Crusoe was horrified to find human bones scattered about the shore, evidently the remains of a savage feast. He was plagued again with new fears. He explored the nature of cannibalism and debated his right to interfere with the customs of another race.

Crusoe was cautious for several years, but encountered nothing more to alarm him. He found a cave, which he used as a storage room, and in December of the same year, he spied cannibals sitting around a campfire. He did not see them again for quite some time.

Later, Crusoe saw a ship in distress, but everyone was already drowned on the ship and Crusoe remained companionless. However, he was able to take many provisions from this newly wrecked ship. Sometime later, cannibals landed on the island and a victim escaped. Crusoe saved his life, named him Friday, and taught him English. Friday soon became Crusoe's humble and devoted slave.

Crusoe and Friday made plans to leave the island and, accordingly, they built another boat. Crusoe also undertook Friday's religious education, converting the savage into a Protestant. Their voyage was postponed due to the return of the savages. This time it was necessary to attack the cannibals in order to save two prisoners since one was a white man. The white man was a Spaniard and the other was Friday's father. Later the four of them planned a voyage to the mainland to rescue sixteen compatriots of the Spaniard. First, however, they built up their food supply to assure enough food for the extra people. Crusoe and Friday agreed to wait on the island while the Spaniard and Friday's father brought back the other men.

A week later, they spied a ship but they quickly learned that there had been a mutiny on board. By devious means, Crusoe and Friday rescued the captain and two other men, and after much scheming, regained control of the ship. The grateful captain gave Crusoe many gifts and took him and Friday back to England. Some of the rebel crewmen were left marooned on the island.

Crusoe returned to England and found that in his absence he had become a wealthy man. After going to Lisbon to handle some of his affairs,

Crusoe began an overland journey back to England. Crusoe and his company encountered many hardships in crossing the mountains, but they finally arrived safely in England. Crusoe sold his plantation in Brazil for a good price, married, and had three children. Finally, however, he was persuaded to go on yet another voyage, and he visited his old island, where there were promises of new adventures to be found in a later account.

SUMMARIES AND COMMENTARIES

Chapter 1: I Go to Sea

Summary

Robinson Crusoe, the narrator of the story, tells us that he was born in 1632 in the city of York, England. His father, a German immigrant, married a woman whose name was Robinson, and his real name was Robinson Kreutznaer, but due to the natural corruption of languages, the family now writes their name "Crusoe." He was the third son; his oldest brother was killed in a war, and the next son simply disappeared.

When Robinson Crusoe first had an urge to go to sea, his father lectured him upon the importance of staying home and being content with his "middle station" in life. His father maintained that the "middle station had the fewest disasters and was not exposed to so many vicissitudes as the higher or lower part of mankind." After his father expressly forbade him to go to sea, and, furthermore, promised to do good things for him if he stayed home, for another whole year, Robinson Crusoe stayed at home, but he constantly thought of adventures upon the high sea. He tried to enlist the aid of his mother, pointing out that he was now eighteen years old and if he did not like the sea, he could work diligently and make up for the time he might lose while at sea. She refused to help him, even though she did report his strong feelings to her husband.

When Robinson was nineteen, on the first of September, in 1651, he joined a friend on a ship bound for London, without consulting either his father or mother. Almost immediately, "the wind began to blow, and the sea to rise in a most frightful manner." Robinson Crusoe, who had never been to sea before, saw this as a sign that he was justly "overtaken by the judgement of Heaven" for his wicked leaving of his father's house without letting anyone know. He was so frightened that he made the promise: "If it would please God here to spare my life in this one voyage, if ever I got once my foot upon dry land again, I would go directly home to my father, and never set it into a ship again while I lived." The wind soon abated, and the next morning the sea was so calm and so beautiful that he entirely forgot the vows and promises that he had made in his distress, and joined the other sailors in a drinking bout.

As they neared a place called Yarmouth Roads, the winds ceased to blow and thus they were stilled for eight days, and when the winds did begin to blow, the ship immediately encountered a storm much more violent than the earlier one. Even the most experienced sailors were down on their knees praying. The storm continued with such fury that the seamen acknowledged that they had never known a worse one. When the boat sprung a leak, Robinson was ordered below to help pump the water. It soon became apparent that they would not be able to save the ship and the captain fired several volleys of distress signals. A lighter ship in the vicinity made it up to their ship and was able to take the crew away from the sinking ship, which foundered soon after they left.

The crew finally got to shore, where Robinson Crusoe met his friend's father, who owned the ship. When the captain heard Robinson Crusoe's story, he felt strongly that it was the "hand of Providence" instructing Robinson Crusoe never to go to sea any more. He told the young man: "You ought to take this for a plain and visible token that you are not to be a seafaring man." He even wondered if he had done something wrong that such a person as Robinson Crusoe should "come onto his ship," and he warned Crusoe again that "you will meet with nothing but disasters and disappointments" if he did not go back to his father's house.

Commentary

The impetus for the idea for *Robinson Crusoe* came to Defoe from his reading of the account of a man named Alexander Selkirk who, in a fit of anger, had himself put ashore on a deserted island. Earlier, Selkirk had gotten into a fight with a fellow crewsman and had himself and his effects put ashore on an island outside of Chili. When he realized the effect of his actions, he pleaded with his shipmates to come back for him, but it was too late. He was marooned on the island for four and a half years. When he was later rescued, the report states that he could hardly speak any more, but he did apparently quickly regain his speech.

The account of Alexander Selkirk was published widely throughout England; he was the subject of an article by Richard Steele in the *Englishman,* and an account of his adventures appeared in many other papers. Consequently, Defoe was quite familiar with Selkirk's adventures, and some biographers maintain that Defoe interviewed Selkirk personally, but this is debatable.

Many of Selkirk's activities on his island are paralleled by Robinson Crusoe on his island; for example, Selkirk fed on turnips, fish, and goat's meat; he became overrun with cats, and he had to use his ingenuity to survive, all reflected in Defoe's novel. In addition, Alexander Selkirk's original name had been Alexander Selcraig, just as Robinson Crusoe's real name had been Robinson Kreutznaer.

A clue to one of the basic ideas of the novel is given in the first chapter, when Crusoe's father admonished his son to stay "in the middle station" of life — this station being the one which "had the fewest disasters, and was not exposed to so many vicissitudes as the higher or lower part of mankind." Crusoe's pride would not allow him to remain in this "middle station." So Crusoe, like the protagonists in many Greek myths and dramas, suffers from the sin of hubris and is accordingly punished. Often during his confinement on the island, Crusoe is reminded of his father's advice and rues his own impulsiveness. Furthermore, the father's pronouncement that his "boy might be happy if he would stay at home, but if he goes abroad, he will be the most miserable wretch that was ever born" becomes a prophetic statement which foreshadows Crusoe's later predicament.

The father's prediction comes true sooner than even Crusoe could expect. His first boat founders and Crusoe makes solemn vows in a time of trouble, but as soon as the trouble is over, he forgets his vows. Thus, we have his first reneging in his word to God. Throughout the rest of the novel, he will constantly contemplate his relationship with God and how much God is punishing him for his "wicked ways."

Chapter 2: I Am Captured by Pirates

Chapter 3: I Escape from the Sallee Rover

Summary

Crusoe, having some money in his pockets, decided to travel to London by land. His decision was based partly on the fact that he was ashamed to go home and face his parents and that his neighbors might laugh at him. In London, he became more and more reluctant to go home and soon put all notion of returning out of his mind.

In London, it was his lot to fall in with some good company. One person he met was the master of a ship which was about to go to the Guinea coast of Africa for trading. The master took a fancy to young Crusoe and told him that he could come along at no expense. Thus, Crusoe entered "into a strict friendship with this captain, who was an honest and plain dealing man." On this first voyage, Crusoe carried forty pounds with him, which was invested in toys and trifles for trading. This was one of the most successful voyages that he ever had since he was able to trade his trifles for five pounds, nine ounces of gold dust, which yielded three hundred pounds.

After they returned to London, his friend, the captain, fell ill and died. Crusoe decided to go on his own again to the Guinea coast and took the other hundred pounds with him, leaving two hundred pounds with the captain's widow for safe keeping. This trip, however, was plagued with misfortune from the first. As the ship approached the Canary Islands, a

Turkish Rover out of Sallee approached them in order to pirate them. They tried to give fight, but their ship had much less fighting equipment and not nearly as many men. The result was that the ship was captured and Crusoe was taken prisoner and carried to the port of Sallee.

Crusoe was not used as badly as were the other members of the crew. He was kept by the master of the ship and was made the master's personal slave. Thus, in a short time, Crusoe changed from a merchant to a "miserable slave." While his new master kept him on the shore to tend to his house when he went sailing, Crusoe constantly thought of his liberty, and, after about two years, he began to design possible means of escape.

When the master would go fishing, he would always take Crusoe and "a young Maresco" with him to row. Crusoe also proved to be an excellent fisherman and was often instructed to catch a mess of fish for his master. Once when they were out fishing, they were caught in a fog and lost their way. Using this as an example, the master had the skiff provided with food and water and also some firearms.

One day, the master was planning on having some of his friends over for a dinner, and he ordered Crusoe to go out and catch some fish for dinner and to bring the fish home as soon as he had caught them. This opportunity provided Crusoe with a way to escape.

As soon as Crusoe knew that he was to have a boat at his command, he began to make preparations to escape. By cunning methods, he convinced the Moor who supervised him to provide the boat with all the necessary provisions for an escape. After pretending not to catch any fish, he told the Moor that they must go farther out to sea. Once there, Crusoe took the Moor by surprise and threw him overboard. He then made the servant Xury swear to be loyal to him and the two of them sailed for five days.

Finally, they were in need of fresh water, and they came into a creek, but there were such terrible animals noises on land that both men stayed on the ship during the night.

When it was time to go for water, Xury volunteered to go so that if wild men came, they would eat Xury and thus Crusoe could escape. Soon, however, Xury returned carrying fresh water and a newly killed animal that resembled a large hare, which they ate with gusto. To the best of his calculations, Crusoe figured that they were somewhere along Morocco's coast in a country known to be uninhabited. During the day, they did see a large beast, which turned out to be a huge lion. Crusoe shot at it and hit it in the leg the first time and the second shot hit the animal in the head. Xury then went to it and finished killing it. They spent the day skinning the animal and Crusoe used the skin "to lie upon."

They sailed on for ten or twelve days, hoping to meet a ship from a civilized country. After about another ten days, they began to notice that the shore was sometimes inhabited, and at other times, completely naked natives were seen waving at them. By signs, they were able to communicate that they had no water and no meat. The natives brought them some dried meat and some corn, which they left on the shore so that Crusoe could come and get it.

While they were lying on the shore, there "came two mighty creatures, one pursuing the other." The natives were terribly frightened and even more frightened and awed when Crusoe took out his gun and killed one of them. The noise of the gun made some of the natives fall down in fear. The other creature was so frightened that it ran away. Being now furnished with dried meat, corn, and water, they sailed away.

In about eleven days, Crusoe spotted land which he assumed to be the Cape Verde Islands. In a short time, Xury spotted a ship with a sail and was frightened, thinking that the old master was after both of them. Crusoe recognized it as a Portuguese ship and sent up a distress signal and also fired a gun. The ship stopped, and in about three hours, Crusoe reached the ship.

The captain, a friendly man, took them in after hearing that Crusoe had been a captive slave. Crusoe offered the captain all that he had, but the captain refused, saying that then Crusoe would be left penniless when they landed in Brazil, their destination. Furthermore, the captain offered him eighty pieces of eight for the boat and sixty more for the sale of Xury. At first, Crusoe was loath to sell "the poor boy's liberty who had assisted me so faithfully in procuring my own." However, when Crusoe told Xury the reason for selling him, Crusoe tells us that Xury was willing to be sold.

Commentary

These chapters continue to fulfill Crusoe's father's prediction that his son will meet with varied misfortunes. Among the misfortunes is his capture by Moors and his subsequent enslavement. Furthermore, his enslavement is correlated to his pride in that he was too ashamed to admit failure and his pride drove him onward to further adventures which result in his capture.

Crusoe's materialism and his acquisitiveness is hinted at in Chapter 2 as he is able to turn forty pounds into a three hundred pound profit. This aspect of Crusoe's character will be greatly emphasized later when he is marooned on the island. There he will collect every possible type of goods, some of which will be of no use to him. Crusoe's materialism and "capitalism" has been the subject of much adverse criticism; it has even been the subject of a critique by Karl Marx.

Chapter 3 describes his escape from his enslavement and it is here that we see the first glimpse of Crusoe's ingenuity, a quality which will be necessary for his survival on the island. This chapter also foreshadows Crusoe's relationship with Friday later on, as it emphasizes his ability to manipulate people and to seemingly win their loyalty as he is able to completely subject Xury to his own will. Many modern critics object to the manner in which Crusoe patronizes people who are inferior to him or who are obligated to him. Others simply refer to Crusoe as an extreme opportunist.

Chapter 4: I Become a Brazillian Planter

Chapter 5: I Go on Board in an Evil Hour

Summary

After a good voyage, Crusoe landed in Brazil twenty-two days later. The captain was very generous with Crusoe, charging him nothing for the voyage and, instead, paying him twenty ducats for a leopard's skin and forty for the lion's skin. Furthermore, by selling all of his goods he made about two hundred and twenty pieces of eight.

Crusoe lived with a planter on a sugar plantation for some time and learned the manner of planting. He later purchased as much land as his money would buy. For the first two years, he planted mainly for food, but by the third year, he planted some tobacco and prepared ground for cane. Now he realized that he should not have sold Xury because he was in need of help on his plantation.

Soon Crusoe discovered that he was "coming into the very middle station, or upper degree of low life, which my father advised me to before." He was amused by this fact because he could have stayed at home and arrived at the same position without all of his adventures.

Since his plantation was at a great distance even from his nearest neighbor, Crusoe often thought that he "lived just like a man cast away upon some desolate island that had nobody there but himself." In retrospect, he was thankful for the slight desolation he had on his plantation.

The Portuguese captain remained for three months and, during this time, Crusoe told him of the money (two hundred pounds) which he had left in London with the English captain's widow. The captain advised him to send for one half of his money so that if that half were lost, he would still have the other half left. Crusoe wrote to the widow and had her send the money to Lisbon. He wrote the widow about all of his adventures, and she was so thankful for his safety that she sent the Portuguese captain five pounds out of her own pocket.

Crusoe's hundred pounds was invested in English goods, which the captain brought safely to Brazil. And instead of buying something for himself with the five pounds, he bought Crusoe an indentured servant. Crusoe was able to sell much of the goods at such a good profit that he bought himself a Negro slave and a European servant.

The next year, Crusoe raised fifty great rolls of tobacco and began increasing his wealth and business. He had now arrived at what his father "had so sensibly described the middle station of life." Having now lived four years in Brazil, and having learned the language and the people, he would often tell his new friends about some of the adventures that had befallen him, especially those adventures along the Guinea coast, where people often bought slaves. His friends were also most attentive to the part of his life that dealt with the buying of Negro slaves. One day, a group of his friends proposed that they would outfit a ship if Crusoe would go to the Guinea coast and bring back a shipload of slaves. Crusoe would get his equal portion of slaves and would not have to contribute to the outfitting of the ship. Crusoe considered this a fair proposal and consented to it.

Having accepted the offer to go for slaves under the condition that his friends would look after his plantation, Crusoe put into writing how his effects should be distributed in case of his death; he left half to the Portuguese captain and the other half to be shipped to England.

After the ship was ready, Crusoe went "on board in an evil hour, the 1st of September, 1659, being the same day eight years that I went from my father and mother at Hull." The ship carried little in commerce, except toys and trinkets for their trade with the Negroes. After about twelve days at sea, sailing along the coast before crossing the ocean, a storm blew up and for twelve more days they were tossed about at sea, expecting every day to be swallowed up. During this storm, one of the crew died and the cabin boy was washed overboard.

When the storm abated, they discovered that they were off the coast of Guinea and that the "ship was leaky and very much disabled." After discussing their lot, they decided to head for Barbados, where they hoped to find repairs for the ship before beginning the ocean crossing. However, a second storm came upon them and blew so violently that the ship was cast upon the sandy coast of an island. The waves were so high that they expected the ship to break up any minute.

With great effort, they managed to get a lifeboat into the high waves and everyone boarded it. After rowing part way to shore, "a raging wave, mountain-like, came rolling astern of us," and it upset the boat and scattered all of the men.

When Crusoe was under the big wave, he swam as hard as possible so as not to be drawn back to sea. He was almost out of breath when the wave finally broke, and Crusoe could feel the ground under him. But immediately he saw the "sea come after me as high as a great hill." This wave buried him under twenty or thirty feet of water and carried him a great way towards shore. Twice more he was covered by huge waves, the last one being nearly fatal since it dashed him against a rock. Crusoe held onto the rock so as not to be washed back out to sea and as soon as he could recover somewhat, he ran up the shore with what strength was left in him.

Once saved, he lifted his arms and thanked God. He began to reflect that not one soul was saved except him. After that reflection, he looked about him to see what kind of place he was stranded in. He had nothing on him except a knife, a pipe, and a little tobacco. Since night was coming on and he envisioned himself being eaten by wild beasts, he found a bushy tree and climbed into it, taking along a heavy club in case he needed protection. Being exhausted from all of the violent activities, he fell asleep immediately.

Commentary

Chapter 4 emphasizes further Crusoe's materialism, and he begins to acquire more land, goods, and money. He realizes also that he is now coming into that "middle station of life" which his father advised him to attain in England. As he prospers, he begins to regret the fact that he sold Xury, not because of his feelings for the boy but because he could have been useful as a slave. Consequently, as soon as he has the means, he buys himself a slave to work for him. Thus, in spite of Crusoe's (and Defoe's) seemingly religious nature, apparently both the author and his fictional character embrace the concept of slavery. In fact, Defoe's own attitude is at least ambivalent if not hypocritical in that, morally, he spoke out against people who "barter baubles for the souls of men" and yet he invested heavily in the slave trade and maintained that it was "the most useful and most profitable trade . . . of any part of the general commerce of the nation."

There is a touch of irony in Crusoe's main objection to his plantation — that is, his isolation, the fact that he "had nobody to converse with but now and then his neighbor." Later, the most pleasant thing to Crusoe is the sound of a human voice after about twenty years of hearing no human sounds.

Unable to be content with his fortune, and ever desiring to acquire more wealth, Crusoe once again tempts fate by planning to go to Africa to buy slaves for himself and for neighboring planters. Thus, his materialism is directly correlated to his later plight.

Having bemoaned his sense of isolation on his plantation, once he is shipwrecked and marooned on the island, he realizes that whatever one's fate is, it can always be worse.

Chapter 6: I Furnish Myself with Many Things

Chapter 7: I Build My Fortress

Chapter 8: The Journal—Parts 1-5

Summary

When Crusoe woke up, he found the weather clear and the storm over. The ship had been carried by the tide almost to the shore. He began to wish to board the ship so that he could save some of the things that he could later use. Later, at the tide's ebb, he found that he could come to within a quarter of a mile of the ship and then he realized that if they had all stayed on board that they would all have been saved. This distressed him so much that he began to cry, but he quickly quit and began to make plans to get to the ship.

After surmounting many difficulties in getting to the ship, he pulled himself up by means of a hanging rope. He searched for all the unspoiled provisions. He found many things, including biscuits and rum, which he wanted to take ashore and he began searching for a boat in order to transport them to shore. He used spare yards and several spars of wood to construct a raft. When the raft was strong enough to load, he lowered the cheeses, corn, the seaman's chest and other provisions onto the raft. He then searched and found ammunition and guns for his use, and then made use of the rising tide to navigate back to the shore with his cache.

The tide took him to a small cove and from here he searched for a safe place to stay, protected from wild beasts and other dangers. Climbing to the top of a hill, he discovered that he was on an island which he believed to be uninhabited. He killed a strange fowl only to discover that it was inedible. He spent the rest of the day bringing his cargo to shore and barricading himself for safety.

Since he was unsure whether or not the ship would last another day or whether it would be blown apart by the winds and waves, he made another trip to the ship in order to bring back more tools and arms. On his return, he confronted the first of the undomesticated cats, which later became a nuisance to him.

Using part of the sail he procured from the ship, he made a tent in which to spend the night. He slept well and, the next day, he made another trip to the ship. This time he brought back some bread, sugar, rum, and flour. He continued to visit the ship every day at low tide in order to get more useful things from it. After thirteen days on shore and twelve trips to the ship, he brought back "about 36 pounds value in money, some European doins, some Brazil, some pieces of eight, some gold and silver." He was amused at the sight of the money because he realized that of all the things he brought off the ship, this money would have the least value for him in his present condition.

A storm blew up and blew hard the entire night, and when morning came, the ship was nowhere to be seen, but he was content that he had brought everything back that he could use before the ship disappeared.

Crusoe's first concern was for his own protection and safety against unknown dangers. Accordingly, he decided upon both a cave and a tent to ward off whatever type of dangers that might appear. Not being satisfied with his present location, he decided to investigate other parts of the island to see if he could find a more suitable location to build his fortress. He found a flat place on the side of a hill and determined to pitch his tent there. Using a cable from the ship and his imagination, he made a type of fortification around the tent to ward off dangers. For further safety, he insured that the only means of entrance was by means of a ladder over the top of the tent.

He carried all of his provisions into the tent and covered them with a tarp to protect them from the elements. He went to work digging a cave, but a storm channeled all of his energy into securing the gunpowder so that it would not become wet and, therefore, useless. During this time, he went at least once a day to discover what he could kill for food. On one trip, he discovered goats on the island. He killed a she-goat and her kid followed him back to his tent. He tried to tame the kid, but it wouldn't eat, so he was forced to kill it and eat it.

He realized that he should find a way to make a fire and to find proper fuel to burn. However, he began to muse on his condition; he wondered if his predicament was "the determination of Heaven, that in this desolate place and in this desolate manner, I should end my life." At this moment, he began to question the justice of Providence that would deliver such severe punishment on a person who had never done a great disobedience. Reproving himself for this bitterness, he began to reason with himself. Surely, he had met a better fate than the other ten in the boat who were undoubtedly dead. Counting his blessings, he realized that he had everything needed for his subsistence, particularly his gun and his ammunition. Realizing this, he decided to keep an account of his trials and tribulations. With this thought in mind, he began a journal of his activities, beginning with the day he landed on the shore.

One of the main advantages of keeping a journal daily was the fact that it would force him to keep account of the time of the year. He recorded the circumstances to which he was reduced, and in the form of a ledger, he listed the "evil" that had befallen him, in contrast to the "good" that was also his lot. After reviewing the pros and cons of his condition and, in spite of the horror of his condition, he realized that, nevertheless, God was on his side and that he had much to be thankful for.

After taking stock of all his possessions, he realized that he did not have enough room to move about it. He then began to build a series of tunnels in the cave which would be a type of safe storehouse for all of his possessions. This accomplished, and desiring a few physical comforts for himself, he made a table and a chair, and realized that "by labour, application, and contrivance, I found at last that I wanted nothing but I could have made it, especially if I had had tools." Thus, he made shelves to store things on and other useful items.

After his labors were completed, he stepped back to observe his domain and it "was great pleasure to me to see all my goods in such order, and especially to find my stock of all necessaries so great." Crusoe then recorded in his journal details about his arrival on the shore and recounted how he came ashore, found himself abandoned, and wept for his plight.

Beginning his journal, Crusoe records:

September 30, 1659: he relived the terror of the shipwreck and his heavy fears.

October 1: Crusoe regretted and bemoaned the fate of his shipmates and determined to board the ship to get whatever provisions he could.

October 1 to the 24th: These days were occupied by the many trips Crusoe made to the ship.

October 20: This was the day that the raft overturned, and he had to spend the entire day recovering the goods from the sea.

October 24: This being the rainy season, he spent this day covering his goods to protect them from the rain.

October 26: He found a proper location to build his home and began in the labors of this task.

October 26 to the 30: These days were spent in transferring all of his goods to his new home and fortification.

October 31: He hunted, killed a she-goat, and killed the kid that followed him home.

November 1: He set up his tent and spent his first night in it.

November 2: He arranged his chests and made a second fortification just within the place he had marked out for his first fortification.

November 3: He killed two edible birds and made a table.

November 4: He followed a time schedule every morning, walking out with his gun for several hours, working until 11:00 A.M., eating lunch, napping from 12:00 until 2:00 P.M., and working until evening.

November 5: He killed a cat and kept the skin.

November 6: He took a morning walk and finished his table.

November 7-12: This time was devoted to making a chair.

November 13: The rain alerted him to the fact that he should parcel out his gunpowder so that if some were destroyed, all would not be lost.

November 14-16: These days were spent making little boxes to hold a pound or two pounds of powder.

November 17: He began to dig behind his tent, into the rocks, but he lacked three important tools, and so he desisted from his work and made two of the tools.

November 18: He searched for a tree known as an iron tree in Brazil and shaped a shovel out of it. Unable to make a wheelbarrow, he made a conveyance similar to a hod. All this required four days.

November 23: He spent the next eighteen days widening and deepening his cave.

December 10: Thinking his labors on the cave finished, a great quantity of earth caved in. After this disaster, he worked diligently to get the ceiling propped up.

December 11: Using boards, he spent a week securing the roof; the posts served as partitions in his house.

December 17: He spent this day until the 20th ordering his house by means of shelves and nails on the posts.

December 20: He put his house in order and also made another table.

December 24: "Much rain all night and all day: no stirring out."

December 25: "Rain all day."

December 26: "No rain and the earth much cooler."

December 27: Crusoe went goat hunting, killed one, lamed another and planned to tame it and breed it.

December 28-30: Due to the heat, he spent much time indoors ordering his house.

January 1: It was still very hot and by evening, traveling through the valley, he discovered lots more goats and decided to bring his dog to hunt them down.

January 2: He brought his dog to hunt the goats, but the goats stood their ground and the dog had to retreat.

January 3: He began his fence, but the rains hindering him for long stretches of time, it took from the third of January to the fourteenth of April to perfect. He was pleased that he had built his fence and fortification in such a way that an outsider coming upon the place would not recognize it as something man-made.

As time passed, Crusoe discovered more different types of wild birds and wild game. And he also learned to make things, such as a barrel that previously he thought that it would be impossible to make. Since he had to go to bed as soon as it became dark, he decided to try to make some kind of candle or light. He put some goat's tallow into a kind of dish and made himself a type of lamp.

During his rummages, he found a small bag of corn but because of rats, nothing was left except husks and dust. Needing the bag for something else, he shook the dust out of the bag near a rock close to his fortification. Much to his astonishment, in time, a few green stalks shot out of the ground and later ten to twelve ears burst out. Ruminating on this miracle, he began to believe that God had caused this grain to grow. He began to cry over God's generosity, when, much to his amazement, he spied stalks of rice. Recalling that he had shaken out some husks months before, his religious gratitude began to abate. He saved the ears of corn with the resolve to sow them again, but it was not until the fourth year that he could allow himself to eat any of this, and even then he had to eat sparingly. He also saved the rice for the same purpose.

Continuing with his journal, Crusoe writes:

April 16: He finished making the ladder which he used to climb into his tent and which he pulled in after him, but he was taken by surprise and was terribly frightened by an earthquake, which caused part of his roof to tumble and several of the posts to crack. The ground shook three times and filled him with such horror that he sat on the ground distressed and distraught, thinking "Lord have mercy upon me."

After the earthquake, the sky turned cloudy and the wind rose so that in no time at all "it blew a most dreadful hurricane." Dejected, he ventured back into his tent, but the onslaught of the rain forced him back into his cave. Because of the dangers involved, he resolved to move his tent, which was under a hanging rock and he spent the next two days deciding how and where to move.

April 22: Beginning on this day, when he realized that his tools were too dull to perform the tasks that needed to be performed, he spent an entire week constructing a grindstone for the sole purpose of sharpening his tools.

April 28-29: He spent two days sharpening his tools.

April 30: His bread supply being low, he rationed himself to one biscuit a day.

May 1: Looking out to sea, he saw pieces of the ship which had been blown to shore by the hurricane. But such things as casks of gunpowder were useless since they were completely wet. But, because of the earthquake, the ship was heaved farther upon the land and when the tide was out, he could walk right up to the ship. Although the inside of the ship was full of sand, he resolved to pull off everything that might be useful to him some time or another.

May 3: Using his saw, he cut through a piece of the beam and cleared away the sand, but was forced to stop by the incoming tide.

May 14: Crusoe went fishing, but caught nothing but a dolphin. He dried it in the sun and ate it.

May 5: He cut more beams from the ship and brought them ashore.

May 6: He brought several pieces of ironwork from the ship and came home very discouraged.

May 7: The beams being cut, the ship fell in on itself and was almost full of water and sand.

May 8: With an iron crowbar, he brought back two planks.

May 9: Crusoe went to work with the crowbar again, but everything was too heavy to move.

May 10-14: Crusoe went every day to the ship and brought back a great deal of timber and iron.

May 15: He tried to cut off a piece of lead by means of two hatchets, but as the lead lay in a foot and half of water, his efforts were futile.

May 16: He stayed so long in the woods getting pigeons that the tide prevented him from going to the ship that day.

May 17: A piece of the head of the ship was blown nearly two miles off, but it was too heavy for him to bring to his place.

May 24: Every day, for about three weeks, he worked on the ship and brought back casks and seamen's chests, but the salt water and sand had spoiled their contents. He continued this work until the fifteenth of June.

June 16: He found a turtle.

June 17: He ate the turtle and her eggs.

June 18: Due to the rain, Crusoe found himself to be cold, which was highly unusual for this climate at this time of the year.

June 19: He was very ill and shivering.

June 20: Violent pains and fever.

June 21: He was very ill, frightened and apprehensive; he prayed to God, but was too sick to know what he said.

June 22: ". . . under dreadful apprehensions of sickness."

June 23: "Cold and shivering."

June 24: "Much better."

June 25: He recorded cold fits, sweats, and fainting spells.

June 26: Recovering somewhat from his illness, he needed food and took his gun and killed a goat, which he ate, and gained some strength.

June 27: The ague came upon him again so violently that he became delirious and cried out, "Lord look upon me! Lord pity me! Lord have mercy upon me!" After the fit, he fell immediately to sleep and awakened later, feeling much better. Falling asleep for the second time, he had strange and terrible dreams. After much horror, he awakened and realized that the last eight years of wickedness "without desire of good or consciousness of evil" had gotten the best of him. He then began to dwell upon his many sins and realized that he acted "like a mere brute from the principles of nature." What gratitude he had felt upon the realization that he was alive after the shipwreck ended in merely being glad that he was alive.

His illness caused him to re-evaluate his thankfulness to God and to reappraise his duty to God. After much soul searching, he cried, "Lord be my help, for I am in great distress."

June 28: After having eaten and refreshed himself, Crusoe went out with his gun but was so weak that he soon sat down and began to think.

Through a series of theological deductions, he decided that God had decided that all of this was to befall him. He then wondered why God had done this to him. Sad and distressed, he went back over his wall to partake of some tobacco for comfort and, in the chest where the tobacco was, he found a cure "both for soul and body." It was a Bible.

Experimenting first with the tobacco, he spent several hours trying to make use of it. Finally, he began to read, and the book opened significantly to "call on me in the day of trouble, and I will deliver, and thou shalt glorify me." These words made a great impression upon him, and he prayed before retiring.

Crusoe then tells us that the "30th was my well day." He killed more fowl and ate more turtle eggs. But, taking more tobacco and rum, he felt worse on the first of July.

July 2: He again partook of his "medicine" and doubled the quantity which he drank.

July 3: He speculated that God delivered him from his sickness, but that he had not glorified Him. Immediately he prayed.

July 4: He began a serious reading of the Bible, beginning with the New Testament. Reflecting on his wickedness, he began earnestly to beg for repentance and came upon more significant scriptures. He began to have hope that God would hear him. So, weighted down with guilt, he came to the realization "they will find deliverance from sin a much greater blessing than deliverance from affliction."

Having regained a measure of peace of mind, he spent from the fourth of July until the fourteenth of July exploring his environment. Having been on the island ten months, he desired a greater knowledge of the physical aspects of the island. It was on the fifteenth of July that he went up to the creek where he first brought his raft on shore and, on the bank of that creek, he found tobacco growing wild. He found several sugar canes also growing wild.

On the sixteenth, he went farther abroad and found several fruits, melons and grapes, and from the grapes, he decided to make some raisins. Spending the first night in a tree, he traveled nearly four miles the next day. He came upon a "delicious vale" and began to believe that he was king and lord of this island, with the right of possession. He also found cocoa trees, orange, lemon, and other citron trees. After spending three days in this pursuit, he went home with samples of all the fruits that he had seen. On the nineteenth, he brought two small bags with him to bring home more. To his surprise, all that he had left in heaps were trodden upon or devoured.

He considered moving his home to that part of the island where it was so pleasant and so fruitful. He spent much of July in this area and built a bower surrounded with a fence, thus becoming the owner of a type of country home. Then great rains came on, which forced him to stay in his seacoast house.

On the third of August, he had excellent raisins, which he kept for winter food. But from the fourteenth of August until the middle of October, it rained nearly every day, sometimes forcing him into his cave for days at a time.

It was at this time that he discovered that his "family" was increasing; his cat suddenly appeared with three kittens, confusing, really, because as far as Crusoe knew, both of his cats were females. From these three cats, he later became so infested with cats that he had to kill them as pests. During the rains, he killed another goat and another turtle and, along with these turtle eggs, the goat meat and the raisins, he had the finest "feast" that he had yet eaten on the island.

On September 30, Crusoe noted that it had been one year since his unhappy landing. He indulged in religious observances and kept a fast, and set apart every seventh day for a sabbath. As his ink was beginning to fail, he resolved to write only of the more remarkable events of his life.

Commentary

The qualities which most readers admire in *Robinson Crusoe* are illustrated in these chapters. Here, we see a man pitted against the forces of nature and forced to use his ingenuity in order to survive. The instinct for survival is, according to some psychologists, one of the strongest of all instincts, and Robinson Crusoe is now reduced to the most elemental existence. Thus the appeal of these chapters lies in the simple narration of how he was able to survive and in his telling of the things that he was able to save from the ship.

Crusoe's materialism is further emphasized as he discovers some money which is of absolutely no value to him, and he recognizes this. However, he is unable to overlook the money and ends up taking it with him. Even when he contrasts the good and evil of his situation, he approaches this as a business man, listing each one as one would enter into a ledger his credits or debits. He is comforted by the fact that his credits are greater than his debits; after all, all of his comrades died in the shipwreck.

Chapter 8 is a long and difficult chapter in which Crusoe goes back in time and reiterates all the things that have happened to him since he landed on the island. There are a few things narrated, but there is nothing highly significant in terms of the entire novel. The main purpose of the journal was to keep track of time, but by the end of the chapter he is running out of ink, therefore rendering this purpose to be of little use.

Chapter 9: I Sow My Grain

Chapter 10: I Travel Quite Across the Island

Chapter 11: I Am Very Seldom Idle

Summary

Having now become aware of the rainy season and the dry season, Crusoe resolved to sow his grain during the dry season. Sowing about two-thirds of his grain, it happened that not one grain came up because of the dry months following. He planted the rest in February, taking advantage of the rains in March and April, and it yielded a good crop. By thus experimenting, he discovered that he could expect two seeding times and two harvests per year.

Taking some time to visit his bower (his summer home), he found to his delight that some of the stakes that he had used in his hedge had grown with long branches so that it supplied him with shade.

After careful observation and bookkeeping, he found that he was able to predict accurately the exact divisions of the year so that he knew reasonably well when he could plant and when he could not. He next learned how to make baskets out of twigs so that he would have containers to hold his harvests. He then endeavored to supply himself with vessels to hold liquids and a pot to boil things in.

Once again, Crusoe decided to explore the island, this time journeying across the island to the opposite seashore. He sees land, which he thinks would not be more than fifteen to twenty leagues away, yet he does not know if it would be the safe land of the Americans or of the Spanish, which would be occupied by cannibals.

He found that this part of the island was much more lush than his own part. On his journey, he caught a young parrot, but it was many years before he could teach it to speak. He also found more she-goats and also some penquins. Even though he realized that this part of the country was nicer than his own, he had begun to think of his part of the island as "home" and he longed to return there.

Fixing a post to mark his travels, he then endeavored to take a different way back, but he soon found himself lost in a large, deep valley. He was forced to return to the pole and come back the way he had gone. In his journey, his dog came upon, and caught, a young kid, which Crusoe brought back to his summer home. After Crusoe returned to his habitation, he spent a week building a cage for his parrot. He then thought of going back to get the kid from his bower. It was so hungry that once it was fed, it became quite tame and followed Crusoe home like a dog.

By this time it was the 30th of September and he had spent two years on the island. He spent the entire day thanking God and cursing his past wickedness. Sometimes at his work, he was struck with despair, seeing himself as a prisoner locked in by the ocean. But he read the Bible daily and believed that God had not forsaken him.

Once again, Crusoe outlined his day, including time for a daily reading of the scriptures. He then describes the work it took to build the shelf, a full three days cutting down the tree. By this, he began to learn the value of patience and labor. It now being November and December, he looked to harvesting his barley and rice.

Fearful of losing his crop to wild hares, he endeavored to enclose his crop with a hedge, but to no avail. He was threatened not only by hares, but also by numerous birds, and he tried to guard his crop with his gun by shooting at the occasional intruders. Drawing on his knowledge of English punishment of thieves, he killed three of the birds and hanged them in chains over the crops, which not only kept the other birds from the crops but made them leave that part of the island altogether.

Having no scythe or sickle, he improvised, using a cutlass, which he had saved from the ship. And even though his crop was small, he was greatly encouraged.

When he made an inventory of all the implements that he did not possess — a spade, a harrow, etc., — he listed the other things which he was able to substitute for implements. He puzzled as to how to make his own bread from his crop of barley and spent the next six months furnishing himself with utensils to grind the barley and bake the bread.

During rainy days, he spent his time teaching his parrot to speak, and this delighted him since he had heard no words except his own since first coming to the island. He also began to experiment with clay, attempting to make earthenware vessels. He made many mistakes in his first attempts, but finally succeeded in making two large jars to hold his corn. With more practice, he turned out little pots, dishes, and pitchers.

His next difficulty was to make some type of mortar so that he could grind or pulverize his grains, and then to make some sort of sieve to sift his produce. Then he needed an oven. This he accomplished by heating earthen vessels on a large fire and baking the bread between the vessels. This took up most of his third year on the island.

His crops increasing, he began to think how to increase his storage areas. Once again when left to his thoughts, he feared all sorts of unknown dangers. The thought of cannibals or of wild animals made him very apprehensive. He looked out to see if anything of the ship was still visible, but saw only her remains. He spent three or four weeks wondering how he could fashion a boat to leave the island. He managed to re-fit the ship's lifeboat, but since it was beached and very heavy, he did not have the strength to launch it into the water.

Commentary

In Chapter 9, "I Sow My Grain," Defoe continues to show us how ingenious Robinson Crusoe is as he is able to master the elements and is able to plant two crops a year, and is also able to master the art of basket weaving in order to have some containers for his harvest.

In Chapter 10, although Crusoe is surrounded with the bounty of the island, he is anguished at his condition: "My very heart would die within me to think of the woods, the mountains, the deserts I was in; and how I was a prisoner locked up with the eternal bars and bolts of the ocean, in an uninhabited wilderness, without redemption." Adam and Eve in a similar garden were banished from it as punishment to show that aspirations and defiance were not acceptable in the eyes of God. Crusoe, on the other hand, was banished to an earthly paradise because of the "wicked, cursed, abominable life I led all the past part of my days."

In Chapter 11, "I Am Very Seldom Idle," Crusoe is seen continuing in his varied activities involved with survival, but he is beginning to expand on the number of things that he can accomplish. By the end of this chapter, Crusoe has been on the island for three full years.

Chapter 12: I Make Myself a Canoe

Chapter 13: I Improve Myself in the Mechanic Exercises

Summary

Taking the examples of Negroes and Indians, Crusoe wondered if it were in his power to build a canoe or a piragua. He chose a tree in the woods and, with much difficulty, cut it down, and began to fashion a kind of boat, but he did not consider how he was to get it to the sea, which was "forty-five fathoms of land away." After five months, he finished the boat.

When he finished his work on the boat, he was pleased with himself, especially since he had never in his life seen either a canoe or a piragua that was made of one tree and was as big as this one. He tried to get it into the water, but it was too heavy to move. He then thought of the possibility of bringing water to the boat by digging a series of trenches, but this endeavor also failed and, with "great reluctancy I gave this attempt over also." This endeavor was profitable because it taught him an important lesson—that is, "the folly of beginning a work before we count the cost, and before we judge rightly of our own strength to go through with it." This work took him through his fourth year on the island.

Thinking again on his condition, he realized that on this island his wants were supplied, he had more materials than he needed to work with, and he was delivered from temptations. He suffered neither from lust, pride, nor greed. He now found his life to be much easier than before, and he frequently admired God's wisdom: "All our discontents about what we want appeared to me to spring from the want of thankfulness for what we have."

He spent entire days meditating on what his condition would have been if he had not been able to save provisions from the ship and if he had not been so plentifully supplied with game. These reflections worked on his mind, causing him to come to a "resignation to the will of God in the present disposition of my circumstances . . ."

He became aware of a strange coincidence of days upon which certain things befell him—for instance, the day he left his father to run away to sea was the same day of the month that he later was made a slave. The next coincidence he recalled was that he escaped from the wreck at Yarmouth Roads on the same day a year earlier than when he escaped from the Sallee. In addition, he was born on the 30th of September, which was the beginning of his "evil life," and he was cast on shore on this deserted island twenty-six years later, which started his solitary and religious life of conversion.

Returning to practical things, Crusoe discovered that he was completely without bread and that his clothes were beginning to decay. Although there was excessive heat on the island, he could not go naked because of the burning rays of the sun. Going through the seamen's chests, he improvised waistcoats and breeches from things found within. He made himself a cap from one of the skins of one of the creatures he had killed. This cap held off the rain so well that he attempted to make a whole suit of clothes from these skins. He then spent a great deal of time making an umbrella.

For the next five years, nothing notable happened to Crusoe. His main occupation was in constructing a smaller boat, one which he would be able to get into the water. At the end of this five-year period, he finally had a boat which he could get into the water and he fitted it with a mast and a sail and began a journey around the island.

According to Crusoe, it was on the sixth year of his captivity when he started out on his tour around the island. At first, he went to a hill and saw a fierce current which he wanted to avoid because it might drive him out to sea. There was the same current on the opposite side of the island, which he also must avoid.

Venturing out on the third day, he found himself almost immediately carried into a current and, fearful that he would be carried far out to sea and die, he reflected on how easy it is for God to make a bad condition worse, and he wished with all his might to be back on his island. Then a breeze came up and maneuvering his mast and sails, he attempted to steer himself toward the island. An eddy carried him back to the northern shore, the opposite shore from which he had left. He fell on his knees, thanking

God, and then he moored his boat in a cove.

Now he was at a loss to know how to get back home. Walking about, he came to a bay and brought his boat there to harbor. Marching along, he found his old bower and fell asleep there. He was startled out of his sleep, however, by a voice calling "Robinson Crusoe, Robinson Crusoe." It was Poll, the parrot, sitting on top of the hedge. He and Poll then returned to their home.

His one attempt at sea so unnerved Crusoe that he lived a very quiet and sedate life for an entire year. Turning his attention to the "mechanic exercises," he fashioned himself a pipe of which he was exceedingly proud. He also improved his wickerware and made many convenient baskets. He then noticed that his supply of gunpowder was fast dwindling and he resolved to hold on to the supply and use snares to catch wild goats and other game and also to begin seriously domesticating some of the goats.

It now being his eleventh year, his first catch included a large "old he-goat, and in one of the other traps, 3 kids, a male and two female." The old goat was so fierce that he was obliged to let it go and he brought only the three kids back with him. He found it necessary to undertake making an enclosed piece of ground to restrain them and to protect them from other creatures. He went about constructing a hedge 150 yards in length and 100 yards in breadth, vowing to enlarge it as the flock increased.

Eighteen months later, he had twelve goats and, in two more months, he had forty-three goats, not counting the ones he had already eaten. Accordingly, he found himself supplied with butter, milk, and cheese. With this bountiful food before him, he praised God for the protection and good things he had received from Him. He imagined himself a king, surrounded by his servants — Poll, his dog, and the two cats — and that everything on the island was at his complete command.

Crusoe resolved to go to sea again, and he describes to us the outfit which he had decided to wear. He wore a shapeless cap made of goatskin, a short jacket made of goat skin, breeches made of the skin of an old goat, and footwear, also out of goat skin. He also carried a goat skin umbrella. He cut his beard, which was once a fourth yard long, and now was very short. Thus, in this outfit, Crusoe determined to make his second sally out to sea.

Observing the current again, he was surprised to discover that the furious eddy which drove him about the last time no longer existed. And since his first piragua was on the other side of the island, he determined to build another one for this side of the island. Perhaps to comfort himself, he made an inventory of all his possessions and of all the creatures that he was "lord" over, and he was satisfied with his realm.

Commentary

In Chapter 12, "I Make Myself a Canoe," Crusoe returns to his contemplations about his fortunes in being removed from "all the wickedness of the world." There he was not tempted by "the lust of the flesh, the lust of the eye, or the pride of life." Yet these thoughts are followed by distinctly materialistic or grandiose thoughts that he was a king or emperor over the island.

In this chapter also, we have one of many inconsistencies of the time sequence. Defoe is not very careful in his plotting of the chronology. In this chapter, at one time, Defoe writes that nothing happened for five years and since he has been on the island four years, this would make it his ninth year, but in a later paragraph, Defoe writes that it "was the 6th of November, in the sixth year" of Crusoe's stay on the island. These are minor inconsistencies and the reader should not be troubled if he cannot work out an exact chronology.

Inconsistencies are also seen in the character of Crusoe. First, he laments his miserable condition on the island and wishes to journey out to sea, then once out to sea, he yearns for his island, calling it a "happy desert." Throughout the novel, he is pleased to be on the island, praising God for having so provided for him and then, at any other given moment, he bemoans his fate and desires fervently to be rescued from his misery.

In Chapter 13, "I Improve Myself in the Mechanic Exercises," Crusoe has so increased his "wealth" and property by the eleventh year of his stay that he can look upon his possessions and say "what a table was here spread for me in a wilderness, where I saw nothing at first but to perish for hunger."

Chapter 14: I Find the Print of a Man's Naked Foot

Chapter 15: I See the Shore Spread with Bones

Summary

After all these years, on an uneventful day, without warning, Crusoe "was exceedingly surprised with the print of a man's naked foot on the shore." He "stood there like one thunderstruck, or as if I had seen an apparition." Confused in his thoughts, he retreated like an animal to his fortification. He could not sleep the entire night because he was so beset by apprehensions. In his confusion, he thought that it was the Devil attempting to trick him in some manner. He dismissed this idea and thought that, instead, it might be a savage from the mainland. He feared that his boat would be found and, thus, his presence on the island would be known. Suddenly, all of his confidence in God left him.

In this uncomfortable state of mind, he finally turned to the Bible for comfort and began to be more rational in his thinking. It occurred to him that the footprint that he saw might merely be one of his own. Even though his mind was not reconciled for weeks or months, yet on the third day of his hiding, the goats needed milking and he had to take courage to go out and tend to them.

Later, becoming more bold, he went down to the shore to measure his foot against the print. He discovered that the footprint was much larger than his own foot. His first thought was to destroy all of his enclosures that he had built in order to prevent being found out that he was on the island. But after considering, he realized that he had not seen anyone in the fifteen years that he had been there, and if anyone had accidentally landed, he had probably gone off again quickly.

He fortified his fortifications with another wall so that now he had a double wall. Concerned with his herd of goats, he resolved to preserve them in a different location. Finding a piece of ground in the middle of a thick woods, he fenced it in to secure his goats. He had still seen no human being, and he had spent two years in his uneasiness. He constantly prayed to God to protect him from danger.

Seeking another part of the island to put more goats, he spied a boat upon the sea. Seeing the boat overturned, his thoughts once again turned toward savages and cannibals. Appropriately enough, as he came down the hill to the seashore, he was horrified to find "the shore spread with skulls, hands, feet, and other bones of human bodies." Crusoe saw a circle "where it is supposed the savage wretches had sat down to their inhuman feastings upon the bodies of their fellow creatures."

Horrified and sickened by this sight, he rushed back to his habitation. Crying, he thanked God that he had never reached this level of degeneracy. It was his hope, having been there almost eighteen years, that he could be there another eighteen years without being discovered by such savages and wretches.

For two years, he ventured no farther than his fortifications, and never fired his gun for fear of detection. But after two years, and after thanking God for his preservation, he turned his thoughts to the possibility of brewing some beer out of some barley which he had grown. Finding no substitute for hops or yeast, he found it was impossible to brew any beer.

Crusoe began to entertain thoughts of how he could execute divine retribution against the savages in case they brought another victim to the island to devour and, thus, save the victim. He entertained several ideas about how he could accomplish this and decided to hide himself in a thicket of trees and ambush the savages.

After describing to us how he armed himself for this attempt, he made a daily foray to the top of the hill to look for boats coming from the sea. As the novelty of this idea wore off, he began to wonder at his authority to determine their fate or to judge their practices. If God suffered them to go unpunished, it could be that they saw no crime in what they did, it being their custom. After consideration, he saw himself in the wrong and decided only to prevent, if necessary, their bloody business and not to attack without provocation.

From a practical point of view, however, he realized that unless he killed everyone who came on shore, he could never be certain of his safety. Presently, he decided to go about his affairs and to conceal himself from them, leaving them to the justice of God: "I gave most humble thanks upon my knees to God that had thus delivered me from blood-guiltiness."

Commentary

The discovery of the footprint in the sand is one of the most famous episodes in all of literature. The general public, however, usually thinks that it is Friday's footprint when, in reality, Friday does not appear for years later. It is never made clear whose footprint it really is, but in the view of later events, we can assume that the footprint belonged to one of the savages of whom Friday was a member. The discovery of the footprint prepares the way for the later appearance of the savages upon the shore and causes Crusoe to be more alert and cautious.

After the discovery of the footprint, two years elapsed before Crusoe had another frightening experience – that is, the discovery of the bones. This event causes Crusoe to contemplate the customs of cannibalism and what his duty should be if he were confronted with the cannibals. He dreams up various plots to kill the savages, yet he soon realizes this possibility: "what authority have I to be their executioner?" Despite this philosophical insight, however, it never enters Crusoe's mind as to the justice of killing many, many people in order to save one unknown savage.

Chapter 16: I Seldom Go from My Cell

Chapter 17: I See the Wreck of a Ship

Chapter 18: I Hear the First Sound of a Man's Voice

Summary

For a year, Crusoe continued in the same mood and, for safekeeping, he moved his boat to a little cove under some high rocks so that no savages could discover it. Apart from his necessary duties, he no longer left his habitation because he still vividly remembered the footprint and the remains of a cannibal feast.

While contemplating God's direction of the universe, he was confused at times as to whether God directed the universe directly or, as Crusoe believed, by little hunches and hints. Since Crusoe was preoccupied with fear for his safety, he no longer invented things or contrived substitutes. He made no fires, lest the smoke give away his presence; he did not fire his gun, fearing that it might be heard, nor did he drive a nail or chop wood, for the same reason — that is, it might be heard. Because he feared to start a fire, he contrived to burn some wood at the mouth of a hollow until it became dry charcoal, which he carried home.

It was while he was cutting wood that he found a large cave, but to his distress, two eyes shined out of the darkness within. Recovering from his fright, he ventured in, with a fire brand only, to find a dying old he-goat. Unable to get him out, he decided to let him lie there, so as to frighten away any exploring savages. Going back to the cave, he found it to be a suitable storage room for guns and ammunitions because the floor was level and dry.

The he-goat suddenly died, and Crusoe buried him inside the cave since he was too heavy to drag out. Crusoe was now in his twenty-third year of residence on the island. He remembered how his dog died, how he taught his parrot to speak more fluently, and how the cats multiplied so fast that he had to start shooting them.

Since it was the month of December, Crusoe went out early to check his fields to see if it was time to harvest, but he was surprised by a fire on the shore. Running back to his habitation, he armed himself with guns for defense and prayed that God would deliver him from the barbarians. After waiting for several hours, he decided to go out and observe the proceedings. He found nine savages sitting around a fire. After a while, they got into two canoes and paddled away. Going down to their camp site, he again found the horrible remains of human bodies. Once again, murderous thoughts consumed his brain, and he was perplexed. Luckily, he did not find a trace of them until May of his twenty-fourth year.

About the sixteenth of May, during a very great storm, Crusoe heard the noise of a gun fired, perhaps from out at sea. Almost immediately, he heard a second shot and decided that it must be a ship in distress. Not being able to help it, he hoped perhaps that it could help him, and so he set a large fire to attract attention. The storm, however, put the fire out. He tried again and left the fire burning all night. The next day, with his gun in hand, he went out to see the ship and saw the wreck of a ship "cast away in the night upon those concealed rocks which I found when I was out in my boat."

Thanking God that he had not met a similar fate, he looked upon the broken bodies and wished that at least one had escaped so that he could have a companion to talk with. A corpse floated up with money in the pocket of the drowned man but, much more important, the coat also contained a pipe. Driven both by a need for possessions and a need for companionship, Crusoe decided to venture out to the boat to see what it held and to see if anyone was alive. Once again, the violent currents were visible. Terrified of being driven out to sea, he hauled his boat into a little creek and sat on the sand with ambivalent feelings.

Determined to get to the ship, he attempted the feat the next morning and, after two hours labor, he finally reached the wreck. From the wreck of the Spanish ship, a half-starved dog swam to Crusoe, which he fed. Boarding the shipwreck, he found the bodies of drowned men and many ruined provisions. He maneuvered two chests onto his boat, some liquor, a powder horn, some brass kettles, and journeyed home, very fatigued. After spending the night in his boat, he awoke refreshed and endeavored to take his treasures to his new cave. Opening the chest, he found no things of great use to him — cordial waters, bottles ornamented with silver, sweetmeats, shirts, handkerchiefs, and three great bags of money and gold bars.

Having stored all these things away, he took his boat to his old harbor and went back to his habitation. He was more cautious than before but went about his business as usual.

For the next two years, Crusoe was preoccupied with schemes to escape from the island. During this time, his mind dwelt upon possible errors which he had committed earlier in his life. First, he realized that he should have followed his father's advice and never left his home in England. Then, if he had not desired greater wealth than was his lot in Brazil, he would never have been shipwrecked, and would now be living a happy and wealthy life in Brazil. Thus, he realized that his greatest sin or error was that he could never be satisfied with his "station in life."

It was obvious to Crusoe that he had created more wealth than he had ever had before, but it was all useless to him. One rainy night in March, being unable to sleep, he again reviewed his life and his present circumstances. Realizing that he was less anxious during his first years on the island before finding the footprint in the sand, he lamented that he had ever been warned of the possible dangers that surrounded him, but thanked Providence for protecting him during all the years that he was naively unaware of the many dangers.

He spent some time trying to understand the habits of the savages that he had seen, and wondered if they were able to come from their land to his shore or if he might not be able to journey toward their land. His thoughts were occupied with travelling to their shore and, only later, did he realize that he never gave a thought to what might happen to him if he did reach the opposite shore — that is, how he would eat, would he be captured by savages, and would he be killed; these, and other dangers, never entered his mind.

Falling into a sound sleep, Crusoe had a strange dream. He dreamed that two canoes bringing eleven savages landed on his shore and that another savage, whom he believed they were going to kill, ran into Crusoe's fortification. Crusoe, smiling and encouraging him, made him his servant. He had the impression that the savage would serve him and guide him from the island. He awoke with such joy that he was disappointed to find that it was but a dream. He decided that the only way he might escape the island was to capture a savage, but he was greatly perplexed as to how to execute this plan.

Hoping the means to resolve this would come to him, he scouted the island every day. After a year and a half, he was surprised one morning by the sight of five canoes on shore. The entire crew of each boat had disembarked so that he had no idea how many savages there were. Climbing to his hill, fully armed, he discerned, by means of a perspective glass, that there were at least thirty men around the fire, upon which meat was cooking. Crusoe perceived that two men were at the mercy of the other savages, one of which was immediately cut open and made into edible portions. The other victim, seeing the savages thus engaged with the butchered prisoner, made a dash for liberty. Crusoe was terribly afraid as he saw the victim running toward him with the entire crew of savages following him. The victim ran so well that, finally, only three men were still pursuing him.

Hindered by a creek, the man swam across, followed by two of the pursuers. Crusoe believed that Providence had provided this opportunity for him, so he advanced upon the two pursuers and fired one shot, which killed both of them. Beckoning to the pursued savage, Crusoe attempted to encourage him to come closer. The savage, dreadfully afraid, advanced, kneeling every so often in gratitude for Crusoe's having saved his life. Crusoe tells us, "I smiled at him and looked pleasantly . . ."

The savage knelt and kissed Crusoe's foot. Suddenly, they perceived that one of the pursuers was not killed but only stunned. Crusoe's savage grabbed Crusoe's sword and decapitated his opressor. By using sign language, Crusoe was able to convey to his savage that they should retreat to his fortifications. And also by means of signs, the savage was able to convey the idea that the dead men should be covered up with sand so that the others could not find them. This accomplished, they headed for Crusoe's habitation. Crusoe then fed him bread, water, and raisins, and the poor creature fell asleep.

Commentary

These chapters constitute a key element in *Robinson Crusoe*. In these chapters, the hero becomes a fearful recluse, regains his self-confidence, and begins to establish, after many years, a friendship with another man. Consider, for instance, how long Crusoe has been on this island: he has had no human contact; he has had no trust in any one. Crusoe has no radio, no stereo, nor T.V. He has only animals, the stars, the sun, and, what has become most important, if sometimes baffling to him, God. Defoe is showing us here that Crusoe is, as it were, a "prisoner" on the island. God has been Crusoe's only "friend" — and yet God — and His will — are elusive. Thus, for a year, Crusoe must live in almost continuous fear — hiding his boat, making no fires, afraid to fire his gun, fearing even to chop wood. He has become, in a sense, somewhat of an animal, constantly on guard for his life. By luck, he discovered a cave, another animal-like dimension of Defoe's narrative description, and lives with an old goat.

Remember, here, that Crusoe has been on this island for twenty-three years. He has had to create new values and new goals for himself and, most important, he has had to find a reason for living. It is human nature to struggle for life, but, after twenty-three years, Crusoe has had to slowly, gradually, and painfully, find psychological and spiritual meaning in his life, and all this time he has been alone and deserted.

Again, as so often, Crusoe, despite his trust in God, is thwarted and confused. Finding savages on the beach, he cannot understand his feelings of wanting to murder them. He is, he ponders, no more than a savage himself. Later, after he has sought for answers within himself and has pondered the Almighty's will, he attempts to signal a passing ship. He fails. Again, he tries to reconcile his futility with his moral realities. Here, a storm — a natural phenomenon — an act of nature, or, conceivably, of God, puts out the fire that Crusoe ignites in order to attract help. Ironically, next morning, he discovers the wreck of the very ship he hoped to signal for help.

In this section, Defoe wants us to feel the panic and anxiety of a man who has been isolated from mankind and from civilization. When Crusoe goes out to the shipwreck, note that he stays overnight on the boat, despite the many soggy, dead corpses aboard. He grabs at small trinkets — many things that he cannot possibly use — gold and silver, toilet water, and bottles adorned with metal lacework. Crusoe is hungry and greedy, needing anything that will reestablish him as a human being and as a man — and not as a savage.

Note too that Crusoe's mind dwells on escape during these chapters. His courage and determination are remarkable, especially when one considers how long he has been on the island. Many people might have given up or perished, but Crusoe has had the physical strength to sustain his life and the moral stamina to accept — even if he questions the justice of — his isolation. And, most of all, he has the hope of freeing himself from his solitary, fearful existence.

Defoe's insertion of the dream sequence may seem a bit contrived by today's literary standards, but when Defoe was writing, works of fiction were relatively new and it was often the custom of alerting the reader to possible later events in a novel by having the main character have a hunch, a premonition, or a significant dream. Now the device has become somewhat trite, but then it sparked a sense of suspense in the reader. Yet even today, when we read about Crusoe's dream of the escaping native and of his flight, we respond to the anxiety within Crusoe. Then, when the dream becomes reality, should Crusoe try to save a savage? Should he hide and avoid being captured and devoured? Defoe takes this opportunity to define his hero as a humanitarian—a wary one, of course, because, realistically, how could he be otherwise? But, most important, Crusoe has, until now, considered his own safety; now he must decide the fate of someone else. He does not make, by conscious choice, but by instinct, what is his Christian duty. He rescues what might be a cannibal, feeds him, and lets him sleep in his fortification. Crusoe has sacrified his safety in order to save, not by definition, a "civilized" man, but, simply, another human being.

Chapter 19: I Call Him Friday

Chapter 20: We Make Another Canoe

Chapter 21: We March Out Against the Cannibals

Summary

Crusoe's savage was "a comely, handsome fellow, perfectly well made, with straight strong limbs, not too large, tall and well-shaped . . . and about twenty-six years of age." In general, his appearance was highly commendable, with an appealing olive complexion. When he awakened, he ran to Crusoe, prostrating himself in thankful submission. Crusoe named the savage Friday to commemorate the day that he saved his life, and taught him simple words like "master," "yes," and "no." Crusoe then gave him some clothes and Friday seemed quite happy to receive the clothes because he was completely naked.

Friday made signs to ask Crusoe if they should dig up the buried men and eat them, but Crusoe, with violent gestures, expressed his abhorrence to that idea. Going to the top of a hill, they discovered that the canoes were gone. Crusoe, armed with his gun, and Friday with his arrows, explored the camp-site. It was a sickening spectacle to Crusoe, even though Friday seemed oblivious to the horror. Pointing to the remains, Friday made Crusoe understand that he was to be the fourth feast, and Crusoe immediately saw the other three skulls and various hands and other bones of the anatomy scattered here and there in grisly array. By means of sign language, Friday told Crusoe that he, Friday, was one of many political prisoners who had supported the old king and the opponents had captured all of his group and taken them to various islands, where it was presumed that all had been eaten. Friday and Crusoe then gathered up all the remains and burned them.

Coming back to the habitation, Crusoe showed Friday how to wear his clothes. Being not entirely at ease, Crusoe put up a little tent for Friday between his two walls. Crusoe also made sure that Friday could not get inside Crusoe's innermost wall without alerting him first. Time, however, was to show that none of the precautions were necessary: "for never man had a more faithful, loving, sincere servant than Friday was to me."

After thanking God for his benevolence and righteousness for sending him such a person as Friday, Crusoe expressed his delight in his new servant, and began immediately to teach him how to speak and understand him. Friday turned out to be a very good and apt "scholar," one that "was so merry, so constantly diligent, and so pleased when he could but understand me or make me understand him."

After several days, Crusoe took Friday hunting and, killing a kid, Crusoe made signs for Friday to go pick up the animal in order to teach him not to be afraid of the gun. Friday, amazed at this weapon, thought at first that it was something to be worshipped. Until Crusoe could teach him to master it, Friday often spoke to the gun, asking it not to kill him. Cooking their game, Crusoe taught him to enjoy the flesh of other animals. Much to Crusoe's surprise, he found Friday getting sick when he tasted salt. In time, he had taught Friday to make bread and bake it. Having two mouths to feed, Crusoe began to make plans to harvest more corn, and he put Friday to work in the fields planting corn.

Crusoe found great satisfaction in Friday's company for the next year, and, during this time, Friday began to understand the English language rather well. Crusoe maintained that he began to love the creature and, in reverse, he believed that Friday "loved me more than it was possible for him ever to love anything before."

Friday explained more fully his capture and how he came to be brought to the island, where he was to be devoured, before Crusoe saved him. Familiar with the surrounding seas, Friday explained to Crusoe the appearance and disappearance of the strange currents. Crusoe asked Friday many questions about the nearby nations and land, and Friday informed him that they could get off the island in a large boat if they had one. Satisfied with Friday's progress in speech, Crusoe undertook his religious education. Friday described his rather simple religion, which Crusoe dismissed as rather heathen.

After listening to a long lecture, Friday asked a question which took Crusoe aback: "If God, much strong, much might as Devil, why God no kill Devil, so make him no more do wicked?" Crusoe, not feeling qualified to answer Friday's question suggested that perhaps God was waiting for the Devil to repent and be pardoned. Crusoe then prayed to God for the knowledge to enlighten this savage.

For three more years, the two men lived on the island. When they did not talk about the scriptures, Crusoe told Friday the story of how he came to live on the island and he told him as much as he could about Europe and England. One time, when Crusoe was showing Friday the ruins of one of the ships that was offshore, Friday remarked that he had seen one like it come to his nation. Friday made Crusoe understand that white men had lived among them. Crusoe wondered if the white men might have been eaten and so he inquired whether or not the white men were still among Friday's people. Friday explained that his nation did not eat its brothers, but only those enemies who came to destroy the nation and were captured.

Some time later, at the top of the hill, Friday spied the mainland across the sea and shouted joyfully "O glad there! See my country, there my nation!" Crusoe became uneasy and worried that if they were to journey back to Friday's homeland that Friday would forget his obligation to Crusoe and have him eaten. For several weeks, Crusoe treated him less warmly than before. To relieve his apprehension, he quizzed Friday at length, and Friday comforted him greatly by saying that his countrymen would learn new ways. Relieved, Crusoe took Friday to his boat on the other side of the island and then they set sail. Friday thought that the boat was much to small to go that far. Accordingly, Crusoe took Friday to the place where he built the larger boat, but had been unable to launch it twenty-three years before. It was so rotten that Friday and Crusoe decided to make a new boat.

Felling a large tree, and working diligently, they completed a new boat in about a month, but it took nearly two weeks to roll it into the water. Friday was quite skillful in his handling of the boat, and Crusoe fitted it with a mast and a sail, which improved its navigation.

It was not yet the twenty-seventh year of Crusoe's captivity, and he thanked Providence, thinking that his deliverance was near at hand. Friday dug a dock for the boat since it was the rainy season and they laid boughs of trees across it for concealment and waited through the rainy months of November and December to start their adventure.

Crusoe and Friday began their preparations for their voyage to the mainland. Once, Crusoe sent Friday out to search for a large turtle, and Friday returned very frightened. He had seen six canoes coming to the shore and feared the return of savages. Using his "perspective glass," Crusoe counted no less than twenty-one savages and three prisoners, and their intent seemed to be a "banquet." He and Friday made plans to kill them all. Once again, he had second thoughts about the justice of his actions and thought that only Friday had the right to interfere since they were his people. Resolving to merely watch and act as God directed, he and Friday hid at the edge of the woods.

Sending Friday to scout, Crusoe found that the savages were already eating the flesh of one of the prisoners and, much to his distress, Crusoe found that the man they were eating was a white man with a beard who had been living among the natives. Observing that they had just sent for another prisoner to be butchered, Crusoe decided that he and Friday should attack to save the poor Christian man, who was about to be butchered limb by limb and be eaten. Crusoe and Friday began to fire on the savages "in the name of God," and chaos reigned as the savages ran hither and thither, screaming and crying. So preoccupied were they with their wounds and their dead, that they provided an opportunity for Crusoe and Friday to run in and save the poor victim, who was lying on the beach. The victim identified himself as a Christian, but was too weak to say much more. Crusoe revived him, partially, with a bit of rum, and gave the poor fellow a pistol to help defend himself against the possible attack of the savages. After much fighting and confusion, four of the savages were able to escape. Crusoe was then able to make an account of all twenty-one of the savages — that is, they had killed seventeen and four escaped.

Fearing reprisals, Friday convinced Crusoe that they should get into the canoe and overtake the savages and kill them, lest they bring back hundreds more and devour them. Jumping into the canoe, they found, much to their surprise, another bound victim, almost dead. They freed him and tried to explain that he was saved. As Friday came near him to speak, Friday discovered to his great joy that the bound man was his father, and he was moved to tears. Crusoe was greatly touched by Friday's expression of affection for his father.

Within two hours, such a storm blew up that Crusoe supposed that the four surviving savages would never make it to the mainland; consequently, they would not fear pursuit. Meanwhile, Friday ministered to his father, giving him raisins, and rum, and a small cake, and then the Spaniard was taken care of. Both former prisoners being extremely weak, Friday made them comfortable in the small boat and paddled it along the shore up to their creek. Since the men were too weak to walk, Crusoe fashioned a "hand-barrow" and carried them to the fortification, but they were at a loss to discover a way to get them over the fortification. Consequently, he and Friday spent two hours making a tent for them outside the fortification, making it as comfortable as possible with two beds of good rice straw and some blankets.

Crusoe once again likened himself to a king. He owned everything on the island, his people all owed their lives to him and were his subjects. Crusoe was pleased with himself that in his "kingdom" he allowed complete religious freedom; Friday was a converted Protestant, Friday's father was a pagan, and the Spaniard was a papist.

Commentary

In these chapters, Defoe describes what most people think about when they hear this novel being discussed — that is, Crusoe's relationship with

Friday. The so-called savage is certainly no Neanderthal type of man; on the contrary, Friday is well-built and handsome and certainly not the hulking, stereotype cannibal. Note that he is eager to learn Crusoe's language and is amazingly adept at learning English. Also he understands, and accepts, if at first reluctantly, Crusoe's adamant abhorrence of eating other men. Friday has a rare sensitivity.

During this period of initial friendship between the two men, Crusoe, as one might expect, is a bit wary of the savage. He does protect him and teaches him English words, and he attempts also to teach Friday certain religious values, but Crusoe is, by nature, suspicious of the young native. Having had no companionship for so many years, Crusoe is torn between a desperate longing for companionship and a fear of the dark-skinned stranger. Because of this, he is hesitant to share his habitation with a man who slaughters men and eats pieces of their bodies. Defoe is very skillful in depicting Crusoe's dilemma. Yet he is never melodramatic; he, realistically, characterizes Crusoe's keeping Friday outside the habitation, making certain that the native could not get inside the innermost wall without Crusoe's being alerted. Crusoe's caution is emphasized in these chapters to highlight the fact that this is an Englishman, a man who is learned, who has lived alone, for many years, with no one to talk to except God. We respond to Crusoe's deep longing to protect and accept Friday as a companion and his fears that, during the night, this stranger might kill and devour him.

In addition to the psychology that Defoe skillfully portrays within the characters in these chapters, there is also an amazing amount of detail that enriches his narrative. Consider, for example, how Friday reacts to his first taste of salt. Crusoe was reared to always salt his food; salt, as a seasoning, has always been one of the most basic ingredients of Western cuisine. Yet Friday is sickened by the spice. Other authors in writing first attempts at this genre, the novel, might have been more concerned with plot. Defoe, however, was always concerned with emphasizing a harrowing event and, then, focusing on minute, telling details that colored his narrative.

In addition to Defoe's careful attention to detail, he was always a superb creator of character, for besides Crusoe's being a "teacher" to Friday, he is also a "pupil." Crusoe learns from Friday about the strange currents around the island and realizes that it is certain that they can escape the island if they are able to construct a boat of sufficient size.

During the first three years that the men share their close friendship, they talk of many things: ships that have come to Friday's homeland, the customs of cannibalism, and, as always, the possibility of escape—and if they could—what would ultimately happen to Crusoe, were he to fall into the hands of a band of natives. Despite Friday's assurance that Crusoe would not be eaten and despite Crusoe's own fears, Crusoe is defiant; he will, with Friday's help, escape. But Defoe is clever in continuing the sense of suspense. He does not take his hero from the island, with the aid of an unlikely, lucky sea current and a deus-ex-machina breeze of the wind; when the two men, after much hard work, are ready to launch their carved, roughly hewn boat, Friday reports that several savages have camped on the island and that the two of them are in danger. This is a brilliant stroke of narrative drama.

Another dimension of Defoe's realism, usually not found in early novels of this era, is revealed when Crusoe assumes a rather smug, egotistical attitude about being a "king" over the natives that he rescues. At first, with Friday, Crusoe was relieved that he had a companion and he was overjoyed, if fearful, and, slowly, he became paternalistic and, finally, he assumed a sense of majesty. Defoe is showing us a very human, if perhaps negative, trait of human nature: man has an assertive, fierce dominance drive. Whereas other writers of Defoe's time were often writing simplistic tales with clear-cut morals and populating their books with "good guys" and "bad guys," Defoe was breaking new ground, creating very real, believable people. Crusoe is a man, composed of both positive and negative qualities; he is isolated and reduced to bare, essential physical and psychological essences. He is as daring, inventive, and as human as Defoe was in creating him.

Chapter 22: We Plan a Voyage to the Colonies of America

Chapter 23: We quell a Mutiny

Chapter 24: We Seize the Ship

Summary

Crusoe ordered Friday to kill a goat and he made a delicious stew with rice and barley. Taking it to the new arrivals, the four of them ate together in the tent, cheered by the meal. Crusoe sent Friday down to the beach to collect the firearms and to bury the dead savages. Using Friday as an interpreter, Crusoe asked the father if the savage who escaped might bring back any more with them. The father's opinion was that they were so thunderstruck at the manner of death that they would assume that it was because of a supernatural power and that they would dare not return.

Time destroying caution, Crusoe once again began to make plans to leave the island. Speaking to the Spaniard through Friday, Crusoe found that there were sixteen more compatriots living on the mainland who would be grateful for escape. Crusoe asked him if the sixteen might be trusted in an escape attempt, adding that he would rather be eaten by the savages than to fall into the hands of the merciless priests of the Inquisition. The Spaniard said that he would make them swear on the Holy Sacraments to be loyal and that he himself would fight unto his death for Crusoe.

The Spaniard proposed that they postpone the trip for six months for good reasons. First, their stock of corn and rice was sufficient for only four, and their stock of supplies should be built up so that when they returned with the others there would be no lack of food. Consequently, the four began planting more seeds and harvesting the crops. They also cut down trees, made many planks with much effort, and, in addition, caught more goats to breed, and cured a large quantity of grapes so that they would have a good supply of raisins. Next, they made wicker baskets in order to hold the harvests. Then, everything being ready, Crusoe sent the Spaniard and Friday's father away to bring back the other white men. They left in October, agreeing to give a signal on their return.

After waiting eight days, Crusoe was awakened by Friday calling, "Master, Master, they are come!" Uncharacteristically, Crusoe ran out without his gun, but presently observed that the boat that was coming was not the boat that they had sent out. Suddenly apprehensive, Crusoe went to a hilltop to see more clearly. He saw what appeared to be an English ship anchored about two and one half leagues away, and the boat coming in appeared to be an English boat. Crusoe was torn with ambivalent feelings. He felt joy at seeing a ship from his homeland, but a hunch warned him to be on guard. What business would an English ship have in this part of the world?

As the boat neared the shore, Crusoe counted eleven men disembarking, three of them bound. Friday thought that the Englishmen were going to eat the others. Crusoe assured Friday that the bound men might be murdered but that they would not be eaten. Crusoe was at a loss to understand the situation and hoped that the Spaniard and Friday's father were near in case of trouble.

Though the three prisoners seemed to despair, Crusoe felt that Providence had brought them here to insure their deliverance because of Crusoe. Eventually, some of the men began drinking brandy and fell asleep. Thus, Crusoe stayed hidden and alert, ready to seize any opportunity to free the prisoners. At two o'clock in the heat of the day, all the men went into the woods to sleep, leaving the three bound men in the sun. Crusoe and Friday approached them and discovered their predicament. The men were astounded at Crusoe's appearance and were so appreciative that they could hardly believe their eyes and ears. Crusoe learned that there had been a mutiny aboard the ship and that the bound men were the captain, the first mate, and a passenger. Crusoe offered to either kill the mutineers or to take them captive. The men decided to take them captive. Accordingly, they all crept into the woods to make plans for the capture.

Crusoe demanded total allegiance to him if he was to help them, and, moreover, free passage to England on their ship. The men agreed readily, whereupon Crusoe armed them. As the seamen began to awaken, Crusoe and his party advanced on them. One man, who cried out to alert the rest, was shot by the other two men. The captain shouted that it was too late to fight and that all should submit to him, return their allegiance to him, and he would spare their lives.

Friday and the first mate went to secure the boat. The captain and Crusoe exchanged stories, learning about each other's circumstances. Later, Crusoe took the three to his fortification and fed them. The captain admitted that he was worried about the twenty-six men that were still aboard the ship, and feared that they would defy them. Crusoe, therefore, schemed to trick them into coming to the island. As they were scheming, there were shots from the ship, signaling for the men to return to the ship. When this failed, another boat with ten men in it was launched and headed for the shore. When they arrived, they were apparently surprised to discover that the first boat had been stripped and that there was a hole in the bottom of it. Apparently thinking that their companions were lost, they started to return to the ship, changed their minds, came back to the shore, and left three men to guard the boat; the other seven began a search for their companions.

After much searching, the seven men gave up and decided to give up their companions as lost and to return to the ship and continue on their intended voyage. In order to prevent them, Crusoe had Friday and the first mate go to a nearby knoll to yell until the crew returned. Friday then left them to go farther into the woods, and Crusoe and the captain surprised the men guarding the boat and after a small scuffle, persuaded them to yield.

Friday and the captain's mate returned and all waited for the rest of the crew to find their way out of the woods and back to the shore. They were shocked to find the boat aground, the tide out, and their companions gone. They began to cry out that the island was enchanted. Taking advantage of the crew's confusion, they waited for them to separate from each other, and then the captain and Friday began to fire at them. Two were killed, and the captain demanded that the rest submit to him, maintaining that he had fifty men with him. Consequently, all the men lay down their arms and professed allegiance to the captain in order not to be hanged. The captain told them that the island was inhabited and run by an Englishman, Robinson Crusoe. Crusoe advised them to be prepared to be sent to England to be dealt with, all except one, named Will Atkins, who was to be hanged the next day because he was the ringleader.

For safety, Crusoe divided the prisoners into small groups and made sure that three particularly fierce prisoners were in the strongest fortifications. As for the rest, the captain talked to them all in order to determine which ones could be trusted, and he told them that he would ask for a pardon if they would swear their utmost loyalty. All humbly promised to be faithful to the captain.

Altogether, Crusoe was able to believe that twelve men were loyal and trustworthy, and he asked the captain if he were willing to take this group and board the ship. Crusoe tells us that he had to stay behind and guard the other prisoners and watch over his "kingdom."

The captain and his men contrived to fool the few men left on the ship by having a man named Robinson yell to them about their difficulties in finding the first crew. Consequently, the men on the ship thought that they were welcoming back their comrades and, consequently, were taken by the captain and his men. Subduing all on deck, they found the new mutinous captain and fired upon him and his accomplices, wounding all of them. Thus the ship was restored to her rightful captain. Signaling to Crusoe on the island, they returned with everything well in hand.

Crusoe, seeing the ship at his command, nearly fainted with the reality of his impending escape. Crusoe remembered to thank God for his deliverance. In appreciation for all that Crusoe had done, the captain of the ship showered many gifts on Crusoe. Then the two men discussed what was to be done with the prisoners. It was decided that Crusoe would grant them a pardon, but leave them to shift for themselves on the island. Crusoe ordered the rebellious captain to be hanged on the yardarm as an example to the rest of the men. Crusoe gave the prisoners much useful information and also told them about the sixteen Spaniards who were to be expected.

Crusoe and the rest of the crew prepared to leave the next day. Two of the five men left on the island swam to the ship's side, begging to be taken on board, and complained about the other three. After being soundly whipped, they were allowed to go along. Crusoe left the island on the nineteenth of December of 1686 and arrived in England on the eleventh of June of 1687, having been gone for thirty-five years.

Crusoe found the widow, to whom he had left most of his money, still alive, but nearly all of his family were dead. Crusoe resolved to go to Lisbon to find out about his plantation in Brazil; Friday, still his faithful servant, accompanied him.

Commentary

After holding us in suspense for several chapters, Defoe at last unfolds the narrative of Crusoe's escape from his long imprisonment from the island. Again, he fills these chapters with such details as how much food Crusoe should take on the boat, the planting of seeds, the harvesting, the cutting down of trees, the goats bred for meat, and the drying of the raisins.

And here again, Defoe tempts us to believe that escape is easy, if one carefully prepares for it. Yet, in the sequence in which the eleven men disembark from their boat, we fear for Friday's life. The boat appears to be

English, and so would not be hostile to an Englishman, even bearded and clothed in skins, as Crusoe is. Yet Friday is a sensitive man—envisioned both by Defoe and by Crusoe. He is no longer a savage; by Defoe's careful plotting and his strong sense of humanity, Friday has become an acute, alert, and loyal friend to Crusoe.

Unfortunately, the escape and the fighting to gain the English boat is accomplished all too quickly, almost in comic-strip sequence. After Defoe has spent so much time telling us about Crusoe's ordeals of surviving on the island, one wonders why he decided to climax the escape so easily. This section is certainly readable, and we are never tempted to put the book down, but the escape is accomplished in a few pages, after much anticipation, instead of a more descriptive, richer finale.

Chapter 25: I Find My Wealth All About Me

Chapter 26: We Cross the Mountains

Chapter 27: I Revisit My Island

Summary

Arriving in Lisbon, Crusoe found his old friend, the captain, who informed him of Crusoe's state of affairs. He told Crusoe that his plantation had done well, and this his partner was still alive. Due to his long absence, Crusoe found his estate in a state of confusion, but one thing was assured, and that was that he had become a very wealthy man. Thus, he began the complicated task of consolidating and restoring his authority over his properties.

True to his old friends, he promised them restitutions for their labors on his behalf when he was in full control of his wealth. After making recompense to the old captain and others, Crusoe had to decide which way to steer his course "and what to do with the estate that Providence had thus put into my hands." He decided first to go to England, but was somewhat apprehensive about going by sea. Acting on his hunches, he decided not to go two different times on two different ships, and this was greatly to his advantage as both ships were lost at sea.

He resolved then to go by land and, taking Friday with him, he and five other gentlemen employed a guide and left for England.

Crusoe and the others set out from Lisbon. Because he was the oldest, and had two servants (Friday being too unfamiliar with this part of the world to serve all his needs), the other men in the troop called Crusoe "Captain."

When they came to Navarre, they were informed that heavy snow had fallen on the French side of the mountains impeding travelers greatly. On arriving in Pampeluna, all were shocked at the extreme cold, especially Friday, who had never seen snow in his life. Because the roads were impassable, they stayed twenty days at Pampeluna. Crusoe suggested taking a small voyage by sea to Bordeaux.

However, before they could act on this suggestion, four travelers arrived, having made it safely through the mountains from France with the help of an able guide. Crusoe and his company employed this same gentleman and, with twelve new arrivals, started out through the snow on the fifteenth of November. Backtracking somewhat, they found themselves in a more commodious climate, entering the mountains from an angle.

Running into some heavy snow, they were warned to be aware of the presence of bears and wolves. One night, as they journeyed in single file, they heard the guide scream out and Friday ran to his aid. The guide had been attacked by wolves but Friday killed one, and the others ran off. The entire company was alarmed. Immediately, however, a bear came out of the woods, which had been chasing the wolves. Although the others made ready to shoot, Friday seemed amused at the sudden appearance of such an animal. Requesting that the others not shoot, Friday assured them that he could "make sport" of the bear, and then kill it. Friday spent much time taunting the bear, making a farce of the bear's clumsy behavior, thus amusing the others. Finally, as the bear was engaged in climbing down the tree following Friday, Friday dramatically pointed the gun at the bear's ear "and shot him dead as a stone." Everyone was amused as Friday explained that this was done for sport in his native country with bows and arrows instead of guns.

Because of the snow, the group hastened on. Entering a forest that they had been warned about, they encountered a dead horse being eaten by wolves. Almost immediately they began to hear wolves baying frightfully. A pack of almost a hundred wolves came at the group. Crusoe ordered the men to form, and they fired volley after volley into the creatures and "hallooed" wildly to frighten them. The wolves went off at a gallop, but during the night they heard them howling and felt themselves watched by wolves in the wilderness.

They also encountered other dead riders and horses and a rider and his horse being pursued by seventeen wolves. As more came out of the woods, Crusoe and his other men laid a line of timber around them and set fire to it. Between the fire and their bullets, at least three score of wolves were killed and many more wounded.

Their guide being ill, they found a new guide and journeyed on to Toulouse and were told by people there that they were exceedingly lucky to have escaped. Crusoe felt that he would much rather go by sea than ever cross those mountains again.

Crusoe arrived safely at Dover on January 14. After praising the old widow for her good care of his effects, he began thinking of going to Brazil. Here, however, he came to a major problem: Crusoe could not decide whether to take up the Roman Catholic religion or be killed in the Inquisition. Deciding to stay true to his principles, he determined that he should sell his plantation. His old friend in Lisbon handled the sale, and Crusoe received a handsome price. He then set up a sum of money to keep the old captain and his son for life.

Crusoe found himself restless; he wanted to travel. For seven years, his friend, the widow, persuaded him to stay at home, and Crusoe raised his nephews. Settling himself, Crusoe married and had three children. At the death of his wife, Crusoe was persuaded by his nephew to go abroad in 1694. Crusoe visited the colony on his island and got the story of the Spaniard's return and their troubles with the prisoners and how, at last, peace was restored. Crusoe brought them necessary supplies and two skilled workmen—a carpenter and a smith. Going on to Brazil, Crusoe sent "besides other supplies, I sent seven women," along with some domesticated or farm animals.

Crusoe then tells us that he went on to new adventures for ten years, which he discusses in a later account.

Commentary

Defore, having delivered his hero from the island, has little else to do but tell "what happened afterward". And, after Crusoe's long imprisonment, he rewards Crusoe with an almost forgotten, but thriving plantation in Brazil. Similarly, Crusoe rewards his old friends generously, and makes recompence to the old captain. The tale could have ended here, but Defoe includes, unnecessarily, the scene with the bear and wolves. One is certain that having survived the rigors of island life, Crusoe and Friday will surmount these dangers, here on "civilized ground".

Mention should be made here of the treatment of women in this novel. Throughout, very little mention is made of females at all. In the concluding chapters, we are told that Crusoe marries, and later sends women to the island. It is interesting, and significant, that we are told nothing of the woman Crusoe marries, and, that the women sent to the island are only as important as the other "supplies". Women, for Crusoe, (and Defoe?) are only mentioned when they are useful to the men involved, or to the plot of the novel. We have encountered Crusoe's, and by extension, Defoe's utilitarianism before in this novel. How does this trait contribute to survival on the island? Can this trait be taken too far?

At any rate, we are promised further adventures, and, indeed, a sequel to this novel appeared, although it is difficult to imagine the aging Crusoe going off in search of new escapades. Probably Defoe merely wanted to cash in on his earlier success.

QUESTIONS FOR REVIEW

1. At the beginning of the novel, what is Robinson Crusoe's attitude towards God and religion?
2. What evidence can you find in Crusoe's youth to determine his capitalism?
3. In your opinion, why did Crusoe want to keep a journal?
4. Compare the ideas regarding man's ability to create, for himself, a civilization in the wilderness in this novel and in Golding's *Lord of the Flies*.
5. What is a "piragua"?
6. How does Crusoe reconcile his urge to kill cannibals with his religious beliefs?
7. In terms of this novel, is "girl Friday" a degrading title?
8. Define Crusoe's paternalism.
9. What are Crusoe's attitudes towards women in the latter part of the novel?
10. How many years was Crusoe on the island?
11. Do you think that Defoe meant this novel to be a moral tale? If so, what was the moral?
12. Is this a "picaresque" novel?
13. Could Crusoe be considered a "racist"?
14. How important were the attitudes of Crusoe's father on his son's development?
15. What trait did you admire most in Robinson Crusoe? What trait did you admire the least?